SCENE STUDIES

By

AMY SHOJAI

And

FRANK STEELE

SCENE STUDIES

Monologues, Duos &
Group Scenes

From

A COMFORT BREEZE
KURVES, THE MUSICAL
STARZ, THE MUSICAL
STRAYS, THE MUSICAL

Shojai & Steele Plays
P.O. Box 1904, Sherman, TX 75091
shojai-steele-plays@shojai.com website: amyshojai.com/plays

Performance rights for all materials contained herein
Must be obtained from Shojai & Steele Plays

A Comfort Breeze © 2008, 2012, 2016 by Frank Steele
Kurves, The Musical © 2011 Shojai & Steele Plays
Strays, The Musical © 2014 Shojai & Steele Plays
Starz, The Musical © 2016 Shojai & Steele Plays
Radio Daze © 2019 Shojai & Steele Plays
Email: Shojai-steele-plays@shojai.com
Website: AmyShojai.com/Plays
ALL RIGHTS RESERVED

Monologues

PUPPY MONOLOGUE (STRAYS)......................9
I LIVE BY NIGHT (STRAYS)........................10
FURRY GIFTS (STRAYS)..............................11
RESPECT (STARZ)..12
TECHIE RAP (STARZ) 13
BROKEN DREAMS (STARZ)....................... 14
FACE of GOD (COMFORT BREEZE).............. 15
DON'T TELL (COMFORT BREEZE)................ 16
HIRING TALENT (RADIO DAZE....................18
GETTING THE GIG (RADIO DAZE)................18

Duos

SHOW DOG (STRAYS)................................ 20
ITCHY DOG (STRAYS)............................... 22
TV'D (STRAYS) 23
NOBODY'S DOG/CAT (STRAYS) 25
FATHER & SON (STARZ) 26
TALK DIRTY TO ME (STARZ)...................... 29
HUSBANDS (KURVES) 30
GETTING A JOB (KURVES) 31
THE GAME (COMFORT BREEZE)................... 33
ENVY (COMFORT BREEZE) 37
PILL BUGS (COMFORT BREEZE) 40
SOUND MAN (RADIO DAZE).........................43
SUCKER (RADIO DAZE)..............................45
WE MEET AGAIN (RADIO DAZE)..................48
I'M A STAR (RADIO DAZE).........................50

Group Scenes

OLD DOGS TALKING (STRAYS) 52
PUFF-PUFF (STRAYS) 54
IT'S TIME (STRAYS) 57
PIANO MAN (STARZ) 59
PERFECT (STARZ) 62
BABY NAMES (KURVES) 64
TOO LATE FOR SORRY (KURVES) 68
YOU WRITE CRAP (RADIO DAZE)..................70
HOLD THAT THOUGHT (RADIO DAZE)..........72

ABOUT THE SHOWS................................. 75

8

PUPPY MONOLOGUE (STRAYS)

PUPPY. So, I'm in the pet store window, watching kids making faces at me, dancing around trying to dodge my own poop, you know...being cute, when this woman comes in. She a big one, too. Looks a little like a beach ball with arms, and I swear, she's singing, "How Much Is That Doggie In The window?" I'm thinking to myself, "Oh, please...not this one. Maybe she's looking at the other window." Well, I look over, and in the other window is a python, so I know she's zeroing in on me.

Well, I'm saying to myself, "OK...I can go with this one. If she's, let's say...portly, maybe she's pretty generous with the feedbag." That might not be bad, and it's gotta be better than gravel they feed me here. So, she picks me up, makes cooing noises right in my face and pays the guy. I'm headed to a new home!

When I get there, it's pretty sweet. A new doggie bed, some nice wet food, a pan of fresh water...yep, I'm gonna like it here. Then comes the rub. "I'd like you to meet Mr. Puff Puff," she says. Mr. Puff Puff is this cat the size of a Volvo and he takes a swipe at me. Luckily I dodge him, but it's hate at first sight. This creep has claws the size of eagle talons, and he looks at me like I'm his next meal. Note to myself: GIVE MR. PUFF PUFF A WIDE BERTH!

Things go along pretty well for the first few days, then comes the naming process. "I'll call you Dinky," she says, which soon morphs into 'Dunkums,' 'Dinkydo,' 'Dinkles,' and my least favorite...'Dinkydoodle.' Well, what are ya gonna do? Every time I respond to any of the new names I get a treat, so I play along.

See, it's not easy being the new puppy. You hafta go through the new trick procedures. First up was 'fetching the slippers.' Now, these things smelled like old Swiss cheese. Did I say "Old?" I mean ancient! Maybe from the first batch ever made. Anyway, I did it. Why? Because I got a treat. Next was 'fetching the paper.' Rain, hail, sleet, or snow, there I was running out like Jesse Owens grabbing a paper that the goofball paper boy tossed in the trees, the flower bed, the grass, the driveway, over the septic tank. I want to say, "Hey, Helen Keller...take aim once in a while. I'm tired of being a mind reader and guessing where you're gonna throw it next." And...again, I did it. Why? Say it with me this time. "Because I got a treat."

Treats are important to a guy(girl) like me. In fact, I delayed my own house-training because the more accidents I had, and the more I got it right, I got a treat.

I heard my person say that I'm going to get fixed! Now, I'm not exactly sure what that is, but if there's a treat involved, it's gotta be good. I'm looking forward to it. Fixed. Yeah, I can go with it. I'm gonna get a treat!

I LIVE BY NIGHT (STRAYS)

PARIAH CAT. I live by night. I have to. Life during the day was a series of dodging BBs, glass bottles, and anything else that could be thrown at me. My question has always been, "Why?" Is it because my coat isn't shiny? My eyes are haunted by fear? My ears are crusty with mites?

That's the appearance. That's what everyone sees.

I look through windows and see other cats being petted, played with, and fed. I see them sleeping on cushions, in chairs, or on beds. Their eyes don't look like mine. They're safe. They're cared for. They're loved, while I eat scraps from the garbage. I'm jealous, and I envy them.

I want to be brushed, scratched under my chin, and I want someone to look at me as though he or she likes me. Is that too much to ask? Am I expecting too much? I'd trade the rest of my lives for one day like that. Maybe for one hour like that.

Here's what no one understands. There is a void in my heart waiting to be filled with love. Yet, my heart is full of love to give.

I live by night, and this night will be like all the others. Sad, seeking security, looking for food, and trying to find a warm place to sleep—the guarded sleep that I've become accustomed to.

If someone or something created all of us, please, please let me be loved. Let me show someone what I have to give, what I have to offer. Let this be the last day I have to drink from puddles in the street. Let this be the day that someone looks past my appearance, and sees what's in my heart.

I live by night....

FURRY GIFTS (STRAYS)

OFFSTAGE VOICE 2. I thank You for allowing me to see in such vivid colors. A scratch beneath the chin, or a tummy rub are the colors of happiness. A catnip toy...maybe a thrown Frisbee, or a kind smile from a beloved human are the colors of joy. A full bowl of food is the color of satisfaction, and a warm place to sleep is the color of peace. Now, if I may, I want to ask that all dogs and cats everywhere might someday see in vivid colors, too. And please let the humans we love—especially the clueless ones—recognize our furry gifts to them. And might that day come soon. Amen

RESPECT (STARZ)

STAGE MANAGER. I'm the stage manager. Also known as the Boss, Ms/Mr Big, The authority, the final say, Almighty Me. This is how I see myself. To the actors and crew, I'm the jerk, the creep, the know it all, pushy son of a (horn). You'll understand that later (or you've heard that before).

I never cared about stepping into the spotlight, but it's not a power trip or shyness that makes me love my behind the scenes job. It's more than wearing headphones and holding a clipboard—it's holding everyone to the highest possible standard. I'm a conductor—just like the one waving a baton to keep the beat going—only I make sure the actors, sets, lights and sound come together in the right harmony. If I do my job right, I'm totally invisible to the audience. But not to my crew.

I'm the first one to show up, and the last one to leave. If I'm a hard-ass (bleep) it's cuz I want the show to be great. And you have to train them right, to jump when they need to. Like this…

PLACES! *(Groups of actors run across stage, total chaos, and stop in pre-assigned spots in poses.)* Am I good or what? *(Costumer sneaks in from the other side to takes place…sewing last bits on a costume).*

It's all about respect. We all want the same thing, and somebody's got to drive the train. I have to earn their respect, though, and it goes both ways. They respect me, but by golly, I respect them back.

Heck, there's no way I could ever sing and dance like *(POINT TO CHARACTER who dances/sings off stage)*, or sew costumes like NAME *(the late comer hands costume to another actor, and they both leave)*, or slap paint and slam a hammer with such artistry *(crew leaves),* shine a light or boost a mic, or create props and makeup effects the audience loves. Yeah, I love my job. And the techies, they're more invisible heroes. But we're all in this together, right?

TECHIE RAP (STARZ)

Why am I here, to support the actor?
We're not just that, it just don't factor.
Got hammers, got wigs, got make-up, too.
Got light bulbs, got costumes, to name a few.

We're big strong guys, and creative girls.
We can deck you out army, or go fluffy curls.
Got nail guns, got drill guns, got big ol' clamps.
Got mics for sound, and great big amps.

I'm tech, ya know, got braggin' rights.
We make actors look good in darkest nights.
Got make-up sponges, lots of powder, too.
Got scary wigs, oh yeah, just try a few.

We're big strong guys, and creative girls.
We can deck you out army, or go fluffy curls.
Got nail guns, got drill guns, got big ol' clamps.
Got mics for sound, and great big amps.

We're tech! let's hear it for all of us.
Mess with us only if you want a fuss.
Got scissors, gaffers tape, and even Elmer's glue.
(sissy voice) I could hurt you, there, actor. Yep, it's true.

We're big, we're strong and the brightest of bright
Running tech gives us lots of braggin' rights.
Mess with us and you will get a fuss,
We're tech, let's hear it for all of us.

BROKEN DREAMS (STARZ)

ADULT ACTOR. What do you do when the dream is broken? Can dreams be broken. Is it time to go away, is it time to pack things in? Should you try for just one more day? I knocked on the show business door for years. Sometimes they opened it just a crack, enough to get a glimpse, but I could never get all the way in. When I was fat, thin people were in. When I lost weight, all they wanted were fat people. I spent years working on accents, going from agent to agent, taking dance (I hate dance, still can't do it), and arguing with vocal coaches whether to character my way through a song or go opera on 'em.

I can sell a song if I have to. I can act with the best of them. And I can cry on cue. But somehow, that's not enough.

I'm through. I've had it. Isn't thirty-five years enough to devote to something. Just because you love something doesn't mean it has to love you back. I'm sad, but it's time to face reality. I'm calling my agent and telling her I'm through. (phone rings) Could that be my agent? Naw, I'm done. I mean, it could be my agent. But why bother. I won't fit the suit anyway.

But wait. What if the suit fits me? For once? I'm going to answer. And pray that this is the one. God, please make it the one.

(*Picks up phone, speaks very quietly*) Hello? (*blackout*)

FACE of GOD (COMFORT BREEZE)

JOETTA. Well, you have questions. Don't you think I have questions? I saw you for ten minutes thirty years ago, and that's it. I have questions, too. Thirty years worth of questions. (*after a long pause*) Well, I saw…Look, this isn't easy for me. I want you to know that. (*going to mix another drink and lighting a cigarette. After another long pause*) Well… Oh, god, here we go. I saw (*Joetta can't look at her*) This isn't going to make any sense at all. It's just gonna sound, I dunno…I saw the face of God. That sounds silly, doesn't it? I saw the most beautiful thing ever created layin' there all wet, and cryin', and wrapped up in this little pink blanket. I saw these tiny fingers reaching out for someone to take hold of 'em. (*starts to cry silently*) I saw this face that had her whole life ahead of her, and I saw this little red spot right in the middle of your forehead, and I was sure, just sure that…well, that was the place where God had put his finger on you, to make everything good for you. You had this little crooked smile, even while you were crying, and it was the smile of the angels. (*she laughs a little*) Oh…and, you were a tough little thing, too. You looked like you were trying to say that nothing and no one were ever gonna stop you. You looked like, "Gimme fifteen minutes, and I'll be ready to take on the world." (*she turns and smiles at Audie*) You looked like you had every secret of life in you, and couldn't wait to tell the world about it. I just looked at you and cried, and cried some more. I couldn't stop. That was the happiest day of my life, and it was the saddest day of my life, both at the same time. Both rolled up into one… both… just… anyway…See, I wanted to buy clothes for you, and show you off, and tell the world to look at you because you were mine. I wanted to laugh with you, and take you on trips, and warn you about anything bad in life. I wanted to see you in your first Halloween costume, and I wanted to make you your first birthday cake for you. I wanted to... to...(*she is sobbing by now*) I wanted you to call me... "Mom"....I just wanted to hear that ONE time. Mom. Was that too much to ask? You were the first thing that was really mine, and no one else's. I saw in you all of the things that...that...I wanted, and...God, help me! Please God, help me through this! (*screams*) God, you son of a bitch! I can't do this! Why? Why? This isn't spoze to be like this! It's spoze to....What did I do? I was wrong. So wrong! Did you hear me? I called God a son of a bitch. I...I...Oh, God help me....Please somebody help me!

DON'T TELL (COMFORT BREEZE)

AUDIE. You didn't' what for me, Joetta? Not a mother? Not a friend? Not someone to come home to everyday? Jesus Christ, I would have come home to you, and Danny, or anyone you were involved with, rather than what I had. You selfish bitch. You decided for me? You decided how I should live? You sailed out of that place in Oklahoma because YOU thought it was best for me? Well, you go to hell. You, and your decisions, and your men, and your damn green-ass luggage. You just go straight to hell. I wasn't the one who got adopted in Oklahoma. Does that surprise you? I wasn't the one people wanted. I wasn't the cute one. Look at me. I don't have looks. I have style, and there's a huge difference. I worked at style because that's all I had. And, you know when I realized it? On my eighteenth birthday. Oh, that's right, on what I

THOUGHT was my eighteenth birthday. I remember now. That wasn't real either, was it? Thanks for telling me. No, I was the one farmed out to foster homes, well-meaning church people, kindly neighbors. Oh, and several influential people in the community. Well, do you know what those people were like? Do you? Except for one family, I was the maid, the dishwasher, the servant, and the sex object. That's right…I figured it up, and I was used as their "toy" one thousand, one hundred, and eighty four times. Those were the fathers, uncles, brothers, and cousins I told you about. I got so I could identify any kind of liquor just by the smell of it on someone's breath. And, you know, I was the one who felt guilty for what they did to me. *(pauses)* "Don't tell, Audilia, God won't like you, anymore. This is our little secret Audilia, only we need to know. Does this feel good, Audilia? Do you like it, Audilia? We'll do it again, Audilia…." *(very calm as she speaks)* I heard that kind of crap as far back as I can remember. Two, three, four times a week I heard it. By the time I was ten or twelve, I just got used to it. I didn't cry anymore. I didn't fight anymore. I knew it was going to happen, so I just laid there and let it happen. I had long since stopped asking God to help me. Two of the men were preachers, anyway. They were "helping" in the name of God….Or, punishing me in the name of God. Take your pick. All I knew was that helping or punishing, it was exactly the same.

HIRING TALENT (RADIO DAZE)

IRVING. The owner's cutting cost every nit-picky way he can. That Bob Hope sure is a penny pincher. *(answers phone)* Hey Roy! What are the chances of getting that girl quartet back? Oh, it's a trio now? Really! Which one. Pedro, huh. She's dead. How did it happen? Really? Niagra Falls in a barrel. Hell yes, I'm going to pay them. Don't I always? Well, last time I gave them something better than money. That's right. Cardboard futures! Not my fault if they can't take advantage of a good stock tip.

This time, I've got something even better. *(almost whispering into phone)* Keep this under your hat. You ready? Mining stock. Zinc is going to be the next big thing. Shhhh, don't tell anyone. There, I paid you in advance. *(long pause)* What in the hell do you mean, you won't send the girls over? Look, I bent over backwards for you, Roy. Okay, it's your loss. And you can tell the girl quartet that it's their loss, too. Oh that's right, I forgot about Pedro. Niagra Falls in a barrel, huh? I'm hanging up, our 30-year friendship is over. I don't want any more contact with you. Hello? Hello? How about that? He hung up on me. *(aside)* Where am I'm going to get a girl trio?

GETTING THE GIG (RADIO DAZE)

DIZZY. *(on phone, angry)* Connect me with Mordecai Waltman. Tell him it's Desdemona Norman. Yes, it's me. Again. No, I don't want to talk to his secretary. Yes, I know he's the head guy. Hey, I'm busy too! Listen, honey, he already promised to get back to me three times this week. I don't care if he told you to hold all calls, that doesn't apply to me. He's my agent, I'm his top client, so technically he works for me. Put him on the phone. *(waits a beat, checking appearance in hand mirror as if he could see her over the phone)* Mordy! What's the deal, booking me into another 3rd rate radio gig? Yeah, sorry about interrupting your meeting *(rolls eyes)*. Okay, sure, I know a job's a job. But my fans miss me! Singing gigs on has-been radio shows isn't my idea of maintaining a career. What happened to that part on the television show, I'm still waiting for my audition slot.

(More angry as she listens). What do you mean, I'm too old? They actually said that? How dare they! *(sarcastic)* Yes, I know the part called for a 25-year-old perky flirty wifey. I can be perky. I can be flirty. I can be 25…with the right makeup and wardrobe. I'm still the DIZZY GIRL everyone loves, dammit! Hell, I've been married four times, so I've got the wifey bit down pat. I didn't even get a screen test. Doesn't experience count for anything anymore? Don't they know who I am?

Get me on television! Just once, and my fans will demand more. Mordy, you're top in the biz, because of me. You've still got pull. So get me my shot, you owe me that much. Yes, I know radio gave me my career, and got me my first movie. But radio's dying. Times change. *(listens)* You could do that? *(grins)* Yeah, in that case, I'll put up with this Podunk radio stuff. Just make sure it's ***sooner rather than later***, Mordy. *(hangs up, doesn't sees PEARL)*

SHOW DOG (STRAYS)

SWAGGER-PUP. I live a wonderful life. I'm pampered, petted, and made a fuss over daily. I travel, and see new things. A lot of people look at me and compliment me. People want to touch me and hold me. I live around others like me who just can't get enough attention. I eat well and have just about everything in life that I want. I'm clipped, brushed, combed and blow-dried. Nothing is too good for me. My people are proud of me, and rightly so...I'm a show dog. I'm elite...one of a kind...the best of the best.

OFFSTAGE VOICE 2. Get a load of THAT guy. The perfect dog...the perfect specimen...a wonder to behold.

SWAGGER. Ya hear that? He's right. I am perfect. (*gives cheesy thumbs-up look.*) My coat shines like a newly waxed car. My ears point skyward as if God himself were calling me. My poses are a study in wonderissity...

OFFSTAGE VOICE 2. That's not a real word!

SWAGGER. It is now, for I can do no wrong. For I wish it to be so...for I AM...ta-daah...Prince Wilhelm Vonprickington Northtarryington Johntarthy Fullbright.

OFFSTAGE VOICE 2. Oh, yeah...well, what do they call you when you're not busy being perfect?

SWAGGER. Dwayne. But, that's only for my few selected friends. Anyway, I thought I'd show you just how it's done, how to pile up the ribbons, how I became me.

This is how to point *(demonstrates).* How to heel *(places hands out like a faith-healer).* I don't have that one perfected. Yet. How to roll over *(rolls over and strikes a pose).* How to stroll the winner's circle *(struts around).* How to be camera ready (*does several over the top faces*).

Yep, it's not easy being me. So many expectations. And, those other dogs! I mean is it just me, or do all wiener dogs smell funny? Don't all Chihuahuas shake? Doesn't every Bloodhound have a face like a melted Eskimo pie? And German Shepherds...all I can say is, "Go find a fire hydrant, Fritz! I'm not impressed."

Oh, I know, you resent me because of what I am. Sure, I'm handsome (*cheesy thumbs up look again).* I'm shiny. I eat like a king. I'm alert. I'm pampered. I'm every dog's dream of perfection, but can I help it? I am...A SHOW DOG. Look upon the perfection of me, and dream...dream and envy...dream and wish.

OFFSTAGE VOICE 2. Hey Dwayne! I just found half a pizza in the trash!

SWAGGER. *(becoming very mutt-like and talking in a goofy voice)* Hot dang! Trash food! One of my...(*aware of who he is*) Oh...I don't know. Who am I, of all dogs, to chase garbage can pizza? I'll look. I mean, what does it hurt to at least check it out? (*walks slowly, nonchalant, to the garbage cans and begins checking them out).*

OFFSTAGE VOICE 2. Wait a minute, Mr. Show Dog, why are you here? How'd Mr. Perfect lose his home?

SWAGGER. *(hesitates)* Not sure. But they kicked me out of a whole city, said my kind wasn't welcome. I think it had something to do with a new musical group came to our town. Ever heard of 'em? The Breed Band? *(dives into garbage can again, comes up with pizza and dashes offstage)*

ITCHY DOG (STRAYS)

SWAGGER-PUP. *(Full of bravado, wanting to hear the older dog's "war" stories.)* Tell me about when the porch fell down. Will ya, huh? Was it exciting? Was it noisy? Were you scared? How'd you get out? I would a dashed out of the way, you know, at the last minute. *(Dancing around, ducking and weaving, fancy paw-work.)* I'm pretty fast, you know.

GLAMOUR-DOG. Scared? Me scared? Who told you that? Nuh-huh, not me. The ground was already wet, that wasn't me. But the noise woke me out of a sound sleep, so loud it hurt my ears. One minute I had a roof over my head—so to speak—and then my world collapsed. Had to tunnel my way out. That's how I got this limp. (*Demonstrates a sexy strut.*)

SWAGGER. (*Delighted.*) You got to *dig*? You lucky dog! I love to dig, I really dig digging. And you had the perfect excuse. Nobody could blame you for excavating to escape. Wow, play and dig and get covered in mud, what fun! What did your people do?

GLAMOUR. (*Pauses*) They didn't know. They'd been gone for weeks. Don't tell anyone, I got a reputation, and it sounds better to say I left them. Hey, don't look so stricken. The neighbor kid made sure I got food every day. I liked that kid. He could sure toss a Frisbee. What an arm!

SWAGGER. Why didn't you stay?

GLAMOUR. My bum leg let me down. I was chasing a Frisbee and somebody grabbed me, tossed me in a truck, and I ended up here. (*Looks around*) Regular meals, solid roof that won't collapse, I got no complaints. Except…I miss that kid. So young fella, what's your story? Did someone leave you behind, too?

SWAGGER. Naw. I had it pretty good. Except for this obnoxious cat named Puff Puff. But after I'd been there a while, I just got this irresistible urge to hit the streets. And my voice changed. No what I mean? (suddenly romantic, puts on an exotic accent). Hey, nice tail...would ya show me your limp again? *(nudge nudge, wink wink)*

TV'D (STRAYS)

PUPPY. What does it mean...TV'd?
KITTEN. What?
PUPPY. TV'd. What does that mean? Is it medicine, or something? I already got neutered, not a lot of fun. See, all I heard the people say one of us was going on TV. That's being TV'd, right?
KITTEN. *(sighing)* No! Gosh, you're clueless. Don't you remember last week. Spike and Mittens got all cleaned up and were gone for an hour, and a little while after they got back—
PUPPY. That's right. People came for them. They made faces, and they laughed and hugged them both. They made some kind of agreement, but Spike and Mittens never came back. They looked happy, though.
KITTEN. Spike and Mittens? Well, they were TV'd.
PUPPY. Spike was on his last hour, whatever that means. And, Mittens...well she looked like she was really ready to get outta here.
KITTEN. She was beautiful, wasn't she? That's what I want to look like. Her head was held high, her coat glistened, and her eyes were so clear. You could hear her purr from clear across the room.

PUPPY. Well, ol' Spike looked pretty good, himself. Soft coat... trimmed claws... tail wagging. Ya know...I never saw his tail wag. The whole time he was in here, I never saw his tail wag. Not until that day. He wagged so hard that he actually fell over. Now, THAT'S a happy pooch! I hope I have a reason to wag that hard.

KITTEN. With that stub of a tail, you're gonna hafta really work at it. (*PUPPY looks dejected*) But, I'll just bet you can do it. In fact, I know you can do it.

PUPPY. *(looking much happier)* Thanks, but I'm gonna wait until I have a reason. You know, I don't want to give it all away, now.

KITTEN. I understand.

PUPPY. Don't take this the wrong way. I don't usually compliment cats, but you look and smell nice. Really nice.

KITTEN. Really?

PUPPY. I'm just saying....

KITTEN. That's because I'm being TV'd today.

PUPPY. Then, why am I here?

KITTEN. I think you're being TV'd, too.

PUPPY. I still don't get it.

KITTEN. I heard the people say something about they take some of us to be on TV, whatever that is, then maybe...MAYBE we get homes.

PUPPY. REALLY! A HOME! You mean like Spike and Mittens? People will smile at us, and laugh and hug us?

KITTEN. Yes. That's what I think.

PUPPY. I'm in. I'm in for the short-haul, the long haul...haul me all over the place. I'm in! What's next? Tell me.

KITTEN. Oh, a bath, a blow dry, a nail trim...let's see...perfume, maybe...

PUPPY. Perfume? Heck, I'd let them rub me with road tar if it would get me a home.

KITTEN. Good luck.

PUPPY. Thank you. You too. And, listen...you really do look and smell really nice. Oh...and do you think the rest of the dogs and cats might get TV'd?

KITTEN. I hope so. If we're really cute, maybe even more people will come here visit the rest of the dogs and cats. Wouldn't that be paw-some? When you really think about it, there's a lot of love that's represented here. A lot of love...

PUPPY. OK. I'm ready. Bring on the bath, the nail trim...even the perfume! Cuz I don't want to stay, I want to go home today. A home where I'm loved.

KITTEN. Me, too...a home where I'm loved.

NOBODY'S DOG/CAT (STRAYS)

OWNER 1. Today I found Nobody's Dog. Her ribs were beginning to show through a once shiny black coat. At first, she tucked her tail tightly and ran, then, ever hopeful, returned with a tentative wag.

OWNER 2. I bet she was cute as a baby. Somebody picked her out special, took her home, and made her believe she would always be loved; but some humans change their minds and their loves as often as dirty socks. Even so, the betrayed black dog is still loving them, futilely waiting for them to come back for her. She had a name once, and now she can't understand, for you see, a pet's love never dies.

OWNER 1. Today, I found Nobody's Cat, one of millions abandoned each year by owners that take the coward's way out. They won't see her slowly starve or freeze to death, be hit by a car, or live at the mercy of strangers as she begs for a scrap of attention.

OWNER 1 & 2. Today, I rescued Nobody's Dog (Cat).

OWNER 2. Finally, she'll be fed, she'll be loved, and maybe she'll be claimed by a more fitting, deserving human into a home where pets are always loved and are never thrown away on a cruel whim. But there are always more cats and dogs, and each still yearns to be ….

OWNER 1 & 2. Somebody's Dog (Cat) once more.

FATHER & SON, PART 1 (STARZ)

SON. (*one side of the stage, to audience*) My name is Percival Wallace Carlson III. Everyone knows me as Wally. I like "Wally." It works for me. My father calls me...

FATHER. (*other side of stage, to audience yells out*) Buck!

SON. (*sighs...*) Buck. Ya know why? It's manly.

FATHER. You're damn right it's manly.

SON. (*sighs again*) My father's known as Percy...not all that manly.

FATHER. My uncle called me Buck.

SON. Whatever....He wants me to man up. You know...be the macho guy. He fishes, watches every sport on TV, and bowls three nights a week.

FATHER. Buck carries a purple book bag...PURPLE! Who does he think he is, Prince? He has a TV in his room, and he watches Dancing With The Stars, and those singing shows where someone wins something. Hey...if the winner got a new rod and reel, I might sign up myself.

SON. Dad and I have this running thing going over Christmas gifts. Last year, I got a football. I gave him a CD of "Fiddler On The Roof." Two years ago He gave me the ESPN sports package for my TV. I gave him the complete recordings of George Gershwin. And three years ago...

FATHER. I got him a catchers mitt...a CATCHERS MIT! And, it was a really nice one, too. He gave me a DVD of "Liza With a Z." I gotta go. "Fishing In The Yukon" is coming on.

SON. I gotta go, too. I'm reading "Pippin" and it's at a really good part. See ya later, Dad.

FATHER. Yeah, see ya. (*looks around*) Where's my Cabela's cap?

FATHER & SON, PART 3 (STARZ)

SON. I know how this sounds. I'm embarrassed to ... wait, I'm not embarrassed at all. I was great. I was everything I knew I could be.

DAD. I hate to admit it...wait, I don't hate to admit it. That kid was great. He sang, he danced, he was...(starting to tear up) well, he was . . .

SON. I hope Dad was proud of me. This was ME, not what he wanted me to be. But all me.

DAD. I still don't get it. I mean, there was talking, I get that. But right in the middle of a good or bad situation, they sing and dance.

SON. I never knew I could sing or dance. Really! But I could. I learned, just like Dad learned to bowl. He's a good bowler. And I'm a real good singer. Dancer, too.

DAD. I've got to let him know how proud I am. There's got to be something…I've got it.

SON. The fact that Dad showed up means everything. I've got to do something…I've got it!

DAD. (crosses to son, sheepish) You were great. I'm so proud…

SON. Thank you, Dad. Thank you for…

DAD. Say, I've got something for you. (pause) It's just a, a little something that (pauses). I mean, you might not want it . . .

SON. I have something for you. (hands program from OLIVER) It's signed, Dad, by everyone in the cast. And…

DAD. Here's a note from you. (pauses to read out loud) "To Dad, my #1 supporter, and my friend." (tears up)

SON. Do you like it?

DAD. More than… (wipes eyes, blows nose). Here. (takes off Cabella's hat) You take this. This is my lucky hat.

SON. (wipes eyes) You wanna hear a song?

DAD. (smiles) You wanna bowl a game?

SON & DAD. (almost unison) Yeah, a lot…a lot! (exit, Dad's arm around Son)

TALK DIRTY TO ME (STARZ)

(The BEEP-sound is an offstage horn timed to cover up the objectionable word.)

OFFSTAGE VOICE. SLATE
LEWIS. Do I really have to read this?
OFFSTAGE VOICE. Please Slate.
LEWIS: Lewis Ray
OFFSTAGE VOICE. This is a make or break part. Whenever you're ready, Mr Ray. I'll feed you the lines.
LEWIS. Ready when you are.
OFFSTAGE VOICE. From page 16. "I want you out of here right now."
LEWIS. Don't tell me what to do, you son of a BEEP. Who in the BEEP do you think you are? I don't have to take BEEP from some BEEP- hole like you. Step outside, and I'll kick your BEEP.
OFFSTAGE VOICE. What page are you reading from Mr. Ray?
LEWIS. Page 61
OFFSTAGE VOICE. No, I said 16. You're reading for the preacher.
LEWIS. I'm so sorry, I'm so embarrassed.
OFFSTAGE VOICE. No problem. Try the preacher, on page 16. I'll feed you the line again. . .
LEWIS. But why in the BEEP didn't you stop me?
OFFSTAGE VOICE. Next!

HUSBANDS (KURVES)

FINGERS. (*To MABEL*) Hey, so you really have four sets of wedding rings? I mean, you said—

MABEL. (*Distracted*) Honey, before I met Reverend Calvin, I thought I was going to have a set for every finger on both hands.

FINGERS. I don't get it.

MABEL. Well, my first husband, Myrtt was…well, we were very young. And, we were very much in love. He wasn't all that nice sometimes, but you overlook a lot when you're in love. We eloped. We saved everything we could and bought this little house, but Myrtt died. He caught pneumonia. I lost the house after that, and I was alone for a while until Newton came along. Newton was older. And he was dashing, so very dashing. (*Wistfully, dreamily*) Our children would have been beautiful—two boys, three girls (*interrupts herself from that lost dream*) I remember he had this tall reddish-brown horse that we both just loved.

FINGERS. What happened to Norton?

MABEL. Newton! Oh, the horse threw him. He hit hard on this rock, and—

FINGERS. The horse hit his head?

MABEL. No! Norton…I mean, Newton hit his head on the rock. The poor man suffered for days, then…Well, I gave the horse away. Newton had a lovely funeral, though. Everyone came. Then I met Jorje'. Jorje' Milton Belew. I guess it was too soon to get married. He was a sweet man, but we didn't have much in common. But, he sang beautifully. He loved to work in his shop, and he would sing Negro spirituals. Oh, to hear him sing "Swing Low Sweet Chariot" was just…well, it would make me swoon. Literally swoon. Jorje' was killed by a teenage driver. The young man was going to pick up his date, and ran over poor Jorje' while he was walking home from the store.

FINGERS. I feel sorry for both of them.

MABEL. Then I married Reverend Calvin. He was a widower who presided over Newton's as well as Jorje's funerals. He was a kind man who had a little money--

MABEL. *(She nods understanding)* Anyway, and he was the one who loved movies. We'd see every movie that came out. We'd go to the picture show every time it changed. We saw them all, and we'd watch them on TV, too. My goodness, how we loved the movies! We had many, many wonderful years, Calvin and I. He went to sleep one afternoon, and he just never woke up. And, do you know what that silly man was buried with?

FINGERS. What?

MABEL. It was in his will that he wanted to be buried with his autographed picture of Gale Storm.

GETTING A JOB (KURVES)

FINGERS. I can do dishes, I can sweep. I can make coffee. Sorta. If it's instant. I can peel potatoes. I can change a tire. I can rake leaves. I can heat up TV dinners, and I'm real careful turning off stoves. Except for that one time, it was an accident. And I can tell you who starred in every movie ever made. Almost. Rio Bravo—John Wayne, Dean Martin, Walter Brennan, Rickie Nelson. Casa Blanca—Humphrey Bogart--

MABEL. Honey, you don't have to sell yourself to me. I've already bought the package. (*Looks at him.*) And you look to be just fine.

FINGERS. Really? And I got a place to sleep? I mean, not on the floor or anything? I lost my blanket—but I kept my lunch box!

MABEL. I think we've got a bed complete with sheets and blankets and even pillows. We'll find plenty for you to do, you'll fit right in with the regulars.

FINGERS. The regulars? (*Looks worried.*) Will they like me? They won't take my lunchbox, will they?

MABEL. We've got rules against lunchbox thievery. There's a mixed bunch, from motorcycle folks to wannabe gang types.

FINGERS. I can rap! (*Starts to rap, badly—beat box sounds*) My name's Fingers and my car's real nifty, drive real fast, cuz it's really swift-y…

MABEL. That's fine, but I think the regulars take care of their own music. Fingers—wait, I can't call you that. Is that your brother's nickname for you?

FINGERS. He's not my brother, I just hitched a ride with him. I wish he was my brother, he's really smart. My momma called me Willy. (*Shy*) Would you like to see my lunchbox? It's got all my treasures. (*Offers it to her*).

MABEL. It's very nice to meet you Willy. I'm Mabel. And I'd love to see your lunchbox.

FINGERS. Can I have a job, too? Please? I don't want to just be a do-nothing. Momma always said, charity is okay but you got to do your part.

MABEL. Your lunchbox tells me everything about you.

FINGERS/WILLY. It does? How?

MABEL. Because everything inside lets me know that you recognize what's truly valuable.

FINGERS/WILLY. Wow. That's neato.

MABEL. It sure is. And because of that, I have a job that only somebody with your credentials could do.

FINGERS/WILLY. Credentials? I have credentials? *(Takes lunchbox back and looks inside.)*

MABEL. We have lots of children stay at the shelter and visit the soup kitchen. And they don't have any treasures. They don't even know what to wish for. You'll be in charge of helping them find their own personal treasure that makes them feel special and happy. It won't be easy but I know you can do it. (Beat) Will you take the job?

FINGERS/WILLY. I could do that! *(With excitement, then very poised)* I would be very pleased to accept the job. I'll make you proud. *(They shake hands.)* I've never had a job. What does it pay?

MABEL. *(Taken aback, then smiles.)* What would you accept?

FINGERS. *(Shy again.)* Do you think—could you maybe sometimes hug me? Momma used to.

MABEL. Oh Willy, everyone will love you. And I'll give you an advance on your salary. *(She hugs him.)*

THE GAME (COMFORT BREEZE)

JOETTA. I've got it. Let's play a game.

AUDIE. Oh, please. Are you serious?

JOETTA. Sure, I'm serious. C'mon.

AUDIE. I'd feel kind of silly playing a game. That's not really why I came here. What kind of game? I mean...

JOETTA. Oh, I dunno...how 'bout 'guess the person'? C'mon, it'll be fun. Just try it, okay?

AUDIE. Guess the person? How do you play that? What's "guess the person?"

JOETTA. I'll think of a person, and you have ten questions to find about who it is. All I can answer is "yes" or "no." Then, it's your turn to think of someone. Wanna play? I've gotta get a drink first, though. (*she mixes a drink*)

AUDIE. I don't know. I really don't play games, and... (*sees that Joetta really wants this*) Okay, sure. I'll try it. I'd rather not, but...

JOETTA. (*sits on the bed*) Okay, I've got someone....

AUDIE. So, what do I do, again?

JOETTA. So, you start askin' questions.

AUDIE. Sure. All right. Is it a man?

JOETTA. Oh, hell yes!

AUDIE. Is he living?

JOETTA. Unfortunately. Okay, I'm sorry. Yes.

AUDIE. Is he famous?

JOETTA. Does a police blotter count?

AUDIE. No. I don't think so.

JOETTA. Then, no. He's not famous. Well...No. No, he's not.

AUDIE. Do you know him personally?

JOETTA. Same answer. "Unfortunately."

AUDIE. How many questions is that?

JOETTA. I dunno, four or five. Keep askin'...C'mon.

AUDIE. Does he look like someone else?

JOETTA. Part of him does.

AUDIE. I know. I know who it is. It's that guy who had the beaded wallet and he looked like Gordon "what's his name".

JOETTA. That's right! It's Danny! And, it's Scott...Gordon SCOTT! And, it was his CHEST, his CHEST that looked like Gordon Scott's. He didn't look like him. Just his chest. Come to think of it, Danny didn't look like anyone. Just Danny. It's sad, too because he always wanted to look like Kirk Douglas. He would even stick himself in the chin with a pencil to get that dimple. You know, that 'thing' Kirk has in his chin? That hole?

AUDIE. *(Laughs)* Kirk Douglas? Did it work?

JOETTA. Hell, no. All he looked like was some idiot with pencil lead in his chin.

AUDIE. Was he the "one"…was he "Mister Right" for you, even with all of the bad stuff? I just wondered because--

JOETTA. Oh, noooo…not at all. Not even in the ballpark. He was just someone to pass the time with. I didn't really even have to marry him. It just seemed like the thing to do, I guess. He made me laugh at a time when I needed to laugh. Do you know what I mean? I just needed a laugh or two. I was coming out of a bad situation…one more of many, and…(*stops herself*) Let's not talk about this right now. It's your turn. Think of someone.

AUDIE. I don't want to play right now. I'd rather…

JOETTA. You've got to play right now. It's your turn. There are only two of us here. I can't very well skip you, and come back later. Now, think of someone. I'll give you five seconds. Ready? Go. (*she looks at her watch*)

AUDIE. Okay, okay…I've got someone. Do I have to play right now?

JOETTA. You're playin'…that's it. Is it a man?

AUDIE. Maybe.

JOETTA. Now, wait a minute. It's either a man, or it's not. Is it a woman?

AUDIE. I don't know.

JOETTA. Please. You're not doin' this right. Damn. Is it a dog or somethin'?

AUDIE. I'm not sure.

JOETTA. Look, I've wasted three questions, and you don't even know what it is? Is it real?

AUDIE. No. It's not real. Not at all.

JOETTA. Then, it's like a cartoon? Is that it? A cartoon character?

AUDIE. I guess so. That's as close as I've ever figured out.

JOETTA. (*getting frustrated*) Okay...it's not a man, it's not a woman, it's not a dog, but it's like a cartoon, but maybe not? And, it's not real? That doesn't make any sense.

AUDIE. I told you that I didn't want to play right now.

JOETTA. Then I give up. I'm usually pretty good at this, too. So, who is it?

AUDIE. I just don't want to say, please.

JOETTA. Look, it's just a silly-ass game. So, tell me. Who is it? Or, what is it?

AUDIE. It's God, okay? God. I thought that would be a good one. And, besides...

JOETTA. Hold on. Wait a minute. You're saying that God's not real? Is that what you're telling me, that you don't believe in God? Hell, EVERYONE believes in God. What's wrong with you?

AUDIE. You believe in God? After all that's happened to—

JOETTA. Hell, yes, I believe in God.

AUDIE. Why? Why do you believe? Just tell me.

JOETTA. Well, because. I mean, I believe in God, that's all... because he...well, because I just do, okay?

AUDIE. Because of the wonderful life you've had? Because you've been so happy, and good things have come to you?

JOETTA. No, not that. Not because of that. I just think that…well, you're s'posed to. That's it. And, if you believe hard enough, then something good's gonna come along, someday.

ENVY (COMFORT BREEZE)

JOETTA. *(angrily)* Now, you lissin, cupcake. You just lissin to me for a minute or two. This started out a little awkward. Then it got okay for a little bit, there. Then, it got real damn awkward again. If I wanted to ride a roller-coaster, I'd have gone the state fair, but not here. Do you understand me? And, what's this "truth" crap, anyway? I don't think you've been honest with me since you came through that door. So, don't give me your speech about truth. You're right. I looked you up. Not the other way around. And, that gives me rights, too. It would have been a hell of a lot easier for you to tell me to fuck off, and not come here at all. So, since you're here, let's talk it out. Let's talk it out, or let's get the hell outta here, and get on with life.

AUDIE. *(coldly)* I'm not used to this.

JOETTA. To what?

AUDIE. Being talked to like this.

JOETTA. Well, pardon me all to hell, but I'm talkin' to you like this. And, I'm not used to tellin' my life story to a complete stranger, either. That kinda makes us kinda blood brothers, doesn't it?

AUDIE. *(after a long pause)* I envy you.

JOETTA. *(shocked)* What? Oh, please.

AUDIE. *(quietly)* I said that I envy you.

JOETTA. (*not comprehending*) Now, why in the world would someone like you envy me? How could you possibly--

AUDIE. Because you ARE real, that's why. Remember when you got so upset because I referred to you as "someone like you?" See, I always wanted to be the one people referred to as "someone like you" but in a different way. That way you just did. That way that means "she's someone special." I guess I wanted to be "something", too. We're not that much different, you and I. (*laughs a little*) I just have nicer luggage, that's all. I have a nicer watch, clothes, car, and a nicer address, but we're the same person. And, I think that's what bothers me so much. I've worked at being better than other people. That sounds terrible, doesn't it? I've worked my ass of for that. All that work, and still....

JOETTA. And, you're still just you. Is that it?

AUDIE. No, I'm still just YOU, and THAT'S it.

JOETTA. (*puzzled*) But, now you've...I mean.... Look, I'm sorry. That one just went right passed me.

AUDIE. Tell me about your mother.

JOETTA. What kinda switch is that? That's not even what we're talkin' about. You were sayin' that we're alike, then all of a sudden, you ask me about—

AUDIE. That's right. Tell me. Tell me about your mother. What was she like? Was she pretty? Was she nice? Was she young, old...what? What was she like?

JOETTA. (*playing along*) Well...well, she was young, but always seemed old. D'ya know what I mean? She was pretty at one time, I guess, but I don't remember her that way. She was always tired. Really, really tired. I remember her always wanting to lie down for a few minutes. Then, she'd lie down for hours. I didn't understand it at the time, but I guess she was always depressed or somethin'. I remember she made the best angel food cakes, though. They were so light you couldn't even feel 'em. She made 'em for my birthday every year. She always just put one candle on the cake, no matter how old I was. She said that was to show me that I was always the one person she loved. Funny, though, we were never close. We couldn't really talk, ya know? She'd just say that I should tell God about stuff, and he'd help me. (*long pause*) I kinda think I'm due a lot of help. Anyway, I loved her, and I felt really sorry for her, bein' married to my dad, and all. But, with all of the crap he caused her, she never talked about it. Even after he took off, I was always waitin' for God to help her, too.

AUDIE. Did he?

JOETTA. No. No, he never did. Not one damn bit. She died not long after you were born. She wasn't that old, either. I think she just died from bein' tired, ya know what I mean? Maybe that was his way of helpin' her. I dunno.

AUDIE. When you got pregnant, did she help you? She must have.

JOETTA. (*starts to cry a little*) No. All she did was take me to Oklahoma and tell me that she'd write me, but she only wrote me one time. She told me that things were fine, and that was it. You know how she signed it? "Your mother"…that's how. Not an "I love you"… nothin'. And, I wrote her every day. After I came back home, after she died, I found my letters to her. They were all unopened. I guess that's when I realized that I was really… alone. All those months, and never a word, never a visit. It's like I'd died. Maybe to her, I was dead. I'm not sure.

PILL BUGS (COMFORT BREEZE)

AUDIE. Don't you know what things were like back then? It's not like now, and I'm sure there were better places, but not where I was. It was a small town, lots of small towns, and… well, it sounds a lot like Eagle Flats. No, care of orphaned kids was different then. The Donagheys really saved me, I guess. At least as much as I was willing to be saved. They had a son about my age, and he was a friend. I guess my best friend. He didn't try to… well, you know. I hadn't thought about it until now, but that was the only time I really laughed. We'd just act silly, you know? Just like twelve year olds do. We called it having laughs with two "f's". It was a nice time, it really was. He taught me to ride a bicycle. He would let me borrow his sister's bicycle and we'd go everywhere. I guess that was the only time I felt safe, when I was with him. His father had this friend I didn't like, though. It sounds stupid, but he was cruel to bugs. You know those little bugs that we used to call pill bugs? Those little armored-looking bugs that would roll up if they were threatened? They were black and, well, we called them pill bugs. I don't know what you might have called them.

JOETTA. Pill bugs.

AUDIE. Anyway, he used to sit out on his patio in the mornings, and eat bags of chocolate chips like you make cookies with. It was cool, and those little bugs would be everywhere. When one would crawl by, he would slowly mash it to death with his foot. He'd just keep eating and talking, and mash those poor bugs. I hated to see him do that. It was just so, I don't know, such a methodical way to kill something. I hadn't thought about that in years, not until now, really. *(pauses)* So, these bugs were just walking to their deaths. I wanted to yell at him to stop, but I couldn't say anything. I just watched, and begged them in my mind to go around, or go somewhere else, but they kept coming, just walking toward him to be mashed into the concrete.

JOETTA. But...why those bugs? Why was that such a big thing with you? It was bad, but--

AUDIE. In one of the places I lived, there was this field out in back of the house. There must have been thousands of those pill bugs. I remember that the first time I was on the honor roll in school there was no one to really tell about it. I just sat in the field and told the bugs that I was smart, that I was on the honor roll. There were no friends, no family, just no one, so I told the bugs. I'd build little houses for them out of sticks, and gum wrappers. They were kind of like, I don't know, kind of like a big family to me. I guess I was maybe ten or eleven. This all makes me sound crazy, but--

JOETTA. No, no it doesn't, not at all. I guess those bugs were to you what my old cat was to me. Sometimes ya just need somethin' to get you through. What happened to the boy? The one you were friends with?

AUDIE. He and his family moved to Montana. His father worked for the government. He was in the Indian Affairs office, and they moved around a lot. I never heard from him after that. They were always moving, I guess. I was shuffled from one town to another... new family... new situation... you know.

JOETTA. Surely, not every family was the same. They couldn't have been...could they? I mean...

AUDIE. Sometimes it was the families, sometimes the people around the families. I was just a way for state money to come in. Nothing more. That's all I was, just an income. Look, I'm not going to go into detail about every person that...well...every person who did things to me. I got past that. It took years, but one day, I finally got past it. Okay, it also took thousands of dollars in counseling fees, but I made it. And, you know something? It all seems like it was someone else, not me that went through it. Experience, my dear woman, is a valuable lesson. Maybe it was for a purpose. Maybe it was…

JOETTA. No it wasn't.

AUDIE. What do you mean?

JOETTA. No one should hafta swim through a mile of shit for a lesson. No lesson's worth that.

AUDIE. No, you're wrong. It made me tough. It made me able to give the world the finger each and every morning when I wake up. That's worth something to me.

JOETTA. Funny, isn't it? I wake up, and think that this may be the day. This may be the brass ring day, and you wake up thinking that once again, no one's gonna screw with me, or there'll be hell to pay from everyone.

AUDIE. Don't give me that. You're the one who looks for water towers.

JOETTA. Yeah, but between the water tower times, I look for something maybe kinda good that I can comb outta life. Can't you do that? Are you capable of that?

AUDIE. (*losing her patience*) This is the life I want! I have everything I want, everything that I--

JOETTA. You have a hole in your heart where honor ought to be. That's what you've got. A great big hole that can't be filled with Rolls Royces or anything else. I'm sad for you. I'm sadder for you than I ever was for myself.

AUDIE. Why? Why be sad for me? I'm over the bad things.

JOETTA. You thrive on the bad things. I can tell that from talkin' to you. You live with bad things and you're gonna make the world suffer right along with you. Roll in the dirt with the rich girl, that's what we're all spoze ta do. Your husband must be--

AUDIE. Leave him out if this.

JOETTA. No. I'm not gonna do it. He must be miserable to hafta--

AUDIE. It's not like that. That's not what we have going.

JOETTA. How does he live with you? Do you give him this ice princes act every day? Does he hafta put up with this?

AUDIE. *(quietly)* He doesn't care.

JOETTA. *(pauses)* He what?

AUDIE. He doesn't care, okay? He has his life. I have mine.

SOUND MAN (RADIO DAZE)

IRVING. We need a sound man. I want the best in the business, the BEST. I sent out 5 letters to five guys who know me and that I've worked with before. I think they'll jump at the chance to get on board with us.

DOTTIE. Oh, I have the responses. I forgot. I had them clothes pinned to the fan on my desk. It makes it sound like a motor-scooter!

IRVING. Fine. Just read the responses. Start with Teddy Thompson. He's the one I want. If he's busy, we'll work our way down the list. Old Teddy...he loves me. *(she opens letter)* I remember when he needed the sound effect of a gate opening in a rain storm. He said, "Who opens a gate in a....." What's wrong?

DOTTIE. Well...he says...

IRVING. Old Teddy...that crazy nut. I remember the time he... What is it? You look funny.

DOTTIE. I don't know if I should read this.

IRVING. Old Teddy.... Go ahead, and don't hold back.

DOTTIE. He says, and I quote: "I remember you, Lipschitz, and I would rather eat a dead vulture than to work with you, again. I'd rather fall off the Chrysler Building than be associated with you. I can't stand you, you son of a..."

IRVING. Yeah, I get it. Must be because of that money he thinks I owe him.

DOTTIE. Why does he think that?

IRVING. Because I owe him money.

DOTTIE. There's more.

IRVING. What else could there be?

DOTTIE. And, I quote: "I've talked to every sound man out there. None of them will work with you, either."

IRVING. My God! You know what that means, don't you? I'm stuck with Rob Bernstein. You know about him, don't you? He drinks.

DOTTIE. So? A lot of people drink.

IRVING. Not like this guy. He eats shredded wheat every morning.

DOTTIE. So? A lot of people eat shredded wheat for breakfast.

IRVING. Yeah, but instead of putting milk on it, he uses bourbon. His idea of a mixed drink is rum, vodka and gin in a large thermos. One time he was so drunk that he was supposed to have gunshots right at the end of radio western.

DOTTIE. And...

IRVING. Instead of gunshots, he had a waterfall and the opening of a coconut.

DOTTIE. So, we can't use him?

IRVING. Are you kidding? If he's available, call him up. Rob Bernstein. We have his number in the files. *(to himself, delays with business)* My God, Rob Bernstein...

SUCKER (RADIO DAZE)

BOB. I know you're wondering why I called you here.

PEARL. Mom said it was important. Of course, everything's important to mom. Except my novel.

BOB. Forget about novel pipe dreams. What was your novel about again?

PEARL. It's gonna be great. It's about a sailor named Buck Rowdy on a torpedo boat. What he really wants to be is a rodeo rider.

BOB. Writer? Like you? What a loser... Well anyway.

PEARL. What do you want, Uncle Bob. Buck Rowdy is a-calling me. When the muse calls, I gotta listen...

BOB. You may not have noticed, Pearl, but your Uncle Bob's dream – this radio station – has seen better days.

PEARL. *(tasting coffee and making a face)* I guess that explains the coffee grounds in the old sock.

BOB. Adds flavor. And you can use it over and over – but I digress.

PEARL. Sorry about the station. What else concerns you?

BOB. I'm using two-year-old weather reports, our advertisers are dropping off like full ticks from a dog.

PEARL. Ew. Hey, can I use that? *(scribbles notes)*

BOB. We haven't had a real star in here since Jimmy Stewart. And he just stopped to asked directions.

PEARL. Why am I here?

BOB. Can you keep a secret?

PEARL. No. Well, yes, but it'll cost you. Mom gives me two bucks a week to keep her up to date on everything. Give me $3 bucks and . . .

BOB. I can give you $1.50 and owe you the rest.

PEARL. *(makes a note on pad)* Okay, sign this.

BOB. Don't you trust me?

PEARL. I know you, Uncle Bob.

BOB. You're the type person would give your book away for free, but charge $5 a pop for an autograph.

PEARL. *(dreamily)* Someday…

BOB. You don't understand. I'm really hurt.

PEARL. Is it your bunions? Your rheumatism? Hemorrhoids? Gout? Did your breakfast back up on you this morning? I told you Mom tells me everything. She talks in her sleep. *(taking notes, to herself)* This is great material!

BOB. No, it's the station, don't you understand? It's WPDQ.

PEARL. What does that have to do with me?

BOB. You pretend to be writer.

PEARL. Really? And you pretend to own a radio station. (*starts to leave*)

BOB. Wait. I need you to write for the station.

PEARL. Write what? A script? About Buck Rowdy? *(starting to get excited)*

BOB. I don't care what you write, as long as it brings in some new advertisers.

PEARL. You want songs? Buck Rowdy is a great singer. I know a song writer can help us out.
BOB. Who?
PEARL. Ever heard of Johnny Mercer?
BOB. You can get Johnny Mercer?
PEARL. I can even get Bob Hope. Wait a minute, did I say Johnny Mercer? I meant Donny Mercer. He's my yard guy and works for donuts.
BOB. Works for doughnuts? That means he works cheap?
PEARL. No, that's the name of the place he works. Doughnuts. What's in this for me? Better be more than a $1.50 and an IOU.
BOB. I know my sister's demanding. It's got to be hard to find time to concentrate on your Great American Novel.
PEARL. Demanding? How would you like to rub lotion on your mother's feet twice a night?
BOB. I've seen her feet. She makes bunions look good. Here's what I can do for you, Pearl. Did I ever tell you you're my favorite niece?
PEARL. I'm your only niece. So again, what's in it for me?
BOB. What would you say to a summer on the coast, with nothing to do but dip your toes in the surf and scribble your Rowdy novel?
PEARL. Sounds like a dream. I didn't know you had a place like that.
BOB. I don't. But I've got a friend of a friend, who knows a guy's cousin, who has a place just like that. I've seen postal cards.
PEARL. So, I just write you a radio play, and you'll fund my summer getaway?
BOB. Is it a deal? It's gotta be good, Pearl
PEARL. (*clears throat, sings a capella*)

HE ROAD INTO TOWN
AND HIS NAME WAS BUCK
HE ROAD A HORSE, CUZ HE
DIDN'T HAVE A TRUCK
TRUCKS WOULDN'T BE INVENTED
FOR ANOTHER 40 YEARS
SO HE DIDN'T HAVE TO WORRY
ABOUT SHIFTING GEARS.
BUCK, OH BUCK, HE'S BUCK,
YESSSERREE THAT'S BUCK
YIPEE-YIPPEE-YEEHAW,
THAT'S BUCK. *(WHIP-CRACK)*
BOB. Now THAT'S a western song!

They shake hands, each holds fingers crossed behind their backs.
PEARL & BOB. *(under breath, TOGETHER)* Sucker.

WE MEET AGAIN (RADIO DAZE)

DIZZY. What the hell are you doing here?
BARRY. *(shocked)* Desdemona Norman! *(gathers composure)* What am I doing here? What am I doing here? Question is, what are YOU doing here, my fair woman?
DIZZY. Cut the crap. That didn't work when we were married, and it won't work now. Shoe polish? Really? Oh, how the mighty are fallen.
BARRY. There's a reason everyone calls you Dizzy. Our marriage was the worse 16 years of my life.

DIZZY. We finally agree on something. Except it was 16 months.

BARRY. When you're in hell, time runs like dog years. Every day felt like a decade.

DIZZY. So how is Wolfie these days? Still 200 pounds of slobbering fur?

BARRY. That was 25 years ago. And he's doing great. I see you're still trying to look like your headshot.

DIZZY. So are you, but with you it's not working. Might try some of that brownish stuff on your head.

BARRY. Ha ha. Shows how much you know. It's Cordovan.

DIZZY. My gosh, you're actually using that stuff? Sad times, Barry, sad times.

BARRY. I heard your career's going great. Last month, a fan letter poured in.

DIZZY. Mordy got me this gig. He's always working the angles, you wisenheimer, so just you wait. But why are you even here? Your career went sideways long ago. I thought you were delivering newspapers. Are you the new Boot Black spokesman?

BARRY. I'm merely incognito. I'm researching a role for a possible play that I'm producing.

DIZZY. Death of a Shoe Polish Salesman?

BARRY. You've heard of it?

DIZZY. Go with your strengths, Barry. Give 'em the performance audiences have come to expect. Hey, it's great reminiscing but I gotta find the director of this dump.

BARRY. Lipschitz.

DIZZY. How dare you!

BARRY. No, that's his name. Irving Irving Lipschitz. But I got here first.

DIZZY. Ladies first, Barry. *(crosses to IRVING's office)*

BARRY. Sure, Dizzy. I always did come in last with you.

I'M A STAR ... (RADIO DAZE)

DIZZY. Okay, Lipschitz, I've got questions, and plenty of 'em.

IRVING. Dizzy please, call me Irving.

DIZZY. Great, Irving. Call me Miss Norman.

IRVING. Haven't you been married 12 times?

DIZZY. None of them counted. My name recognition trumps 'em all.

IRVING. I can see why they moved on...

DIZZY. I'm a star of the first magnitude. They're still talking about my movie, HONEYMOON AT MIDNIGHT.

IRVING. That was followed by HONEYMOON AT BREAKFAST, HONEYMOON FOR LUNCH, and HONEYMOON FOR SUPPER. None of them made a dime and you know it.

DIZZY. HONEYMOON FOR DESERT would have been the biggest of all, if the director hadn't gone on a diet.

IRVING. You say the reviews were in bad taste? But if you believe the sweet ones, you gotta believe the sour ones, too. I remember that one. They said the worst part of the movie was when the projector started. The best part was when the film broke. And if you'll remember, the critic who wrote that was your sister.

DIZZY. Ex-sister.

IRVING. You can divorce your sister?

DIZZY. You've got some nerve talking. (*looks around station*) Is this your pinnacle of success? Hitching your wagon to my star?

IRVING. I've hitched my wagon to bigger asses than you.

DIZZY. Well, I never!

IRVING. Well, you did at least twelve times.

DIZZY. Four, but who's counting. And what do you care, anyway? I'm here to do a job, slumming it, but this isn't what my agent promised.

IRVING. I resent that. WPDQ stands for the best and brightest in entertainment. A lot of big names got their start here.

DIZZY. And I'm gonna get my end . . .

IRVING. Ever heard of Heddy Lamar, Lawrence Olivier . . .

DIZZY. But he's from England.

IRVING. To work here, the boat ride over was worth it. Ever heard of Edgar Bergan, Jimmy Durante, Jack Benny, or your namesake Desi Arnez.

DIZZY. My name is Desdemona Norman, and you know it. Only my friends call me Dizzy.

IRVING. And with your attitude, you can count friends on one finger.

DIZZY. (*muttering*) I'll show you one finger! (*full voice*) Answer me this, Irving. I need top billing, name above the title, payment in advance or you can find another star to float your sinking ship.

IRVING. Those aren't questions, those are demands.

DIZZY. Semantics. Exactly the same, only different.

IRVING. All the A-list stars turned me down. That's why we asked you.

DIZZY. How dare you!

IRVING. Take it up with your agent. You've already signed the contract, baby, so live with it. Don't even think about phoning it in. I have a lot riding on this – a lot of us do – so this isn't all about you. For once in your life, think about somebody else.

DIZZY. Nobody has ever talked to me like that. Except for . . . *(unseen, BARRY enters and watches from sideline)*

IRVING. Then it's way past time. (*exit*)

OLD DOGS TALKING (STRAYS)

DOBERMAN. I used to glide through the air like a fighter jet. Yep, I'd get in position and—

CHIHUAHUA. *(very nervous)* And, then what?

DOBERMAN. Then I'd snarl and bark and slobber and...

BASSET. *(cupping his ear to hear)* Now, wait a minute. No one, and I mean NO ONE can slobber like I can. I practically invented slobbering.

CHIHUAHUA. You can't out slobber a bulldog.

BASSET. What? What's that? My hearing's not what it was, and...

CHIHUAHUA. *(shouting)* I said that you can't out slobber a bulldog.

BASSET. Why would I want to clobber a bullfrog?

DOBERMAN. *(shouting)* BULLDOG! He said, "BULLDOG!"

BASSET. Bullfrog. That's right. I used to catch bullfrogs. They'd wet in my mouth and I'd slobber, and...

CHIHUAHUA. *(to all)* Let it go. Hey, did you see that new Poodle? Just moved into the house down the street. Mamachiwawa...makes me wish I was a few years younger.

BASSET. Who's got a hunger?

DOBERMAN. He said HUN...why do I bother?

BASSET. Are we still talking about bullfrogs?

CHIHUAHUA. Hey, here she comes! Get your noses ready boys. It's sniffing time.

GLAMOUR. Well, hello boys. (*boy dogs start panting, sniffing, etc.*) I'd like to get to know each and every one of you sometime, but (*she winks*) on my terms.

BASSET. (*to all*) What's that? She's got worms? What'd she say?

DOBERMAN. WORMS! She said that she had...wait a minute. Now, you've got me doing it. "Terms." She said that she had terms.

BASSET. Oh, yeah. Worms. I had 'em once. Drug my butt along the carpet for weeks.

GLAMOUR. Is he OK?

DOBERMAN. He's fine. Just a little deaf.

CHIHUAHUA. How about dinner, my little chili pepper?

GLAMOUR. Can't now. Got a date down the street to meet a Bulldog.

BASSET. Gonna eat a bullfrog? Those things'll make you slobber.

GLAMOUR. (*sexy voice, looking at Basset*) OK...well...(*blows them a kiss*) See you later, boys. (*swishes off stage. They all watch her leave*)

DOBERMAN. That's someone I'm gonna get to know real soon!

CHIHUAHUA. Muy bueno! She's hotter than summer pavement!

BASSET. Why the heck would she want to eat a bullfrog? I did that once. Made me slobber real bad. (*to*

Doberman) You were saying something about how you'd glide like a jet, or hated to get wet, or...what were we saying about bullfrogs? Oh, yeah...those things'll make you slobber.

PUFF-PUFF (STRAYS)

PRACTICAL CAT. Puff Puff... Puff Puff. *(No response, she pokes him, finally yells.)* OH PUFF PUFF!

PUFF-PUFF. Will you lay off of that "Puff Puff" stuff.

PRACTICAL CAT. Oh, that's right...(*winks at other cats*) you're, what was it? Buck? George? Raymond? Maybe, Ralph? No, let's see...John Wayne?

PUFF-PUFF. I don't care what you call me. Just PLEASE, NOT PUFF-PUFF!

KITTEN. OK, Dino *(laughs)*.

PUFF-PUFF. "Dino"...Yeah, I like it!

PRACTICAL CAT. Anyway, Puff Puff...you were saying, now what got you out on the streets?

PUFF-PUFF. (*Sighs, not happy*) Well, I still don't get it. Oh, I had a home, but my person was a hard-case I just could not get trained. Sent lots of messages, but she ignored every Pee-Mail note I left. I guess it was about the third time...no, maybe it was the seventieth time that I pooped in the planter that I...

PRACTICAL CAT. You pooped in the planter?

PUFF-PUFF. Yeah, well, anyway...

KITTEN. Why did you do that?

PUFF-PUFF. The planter offered some privacy. And digging ops. You ever try to dig stinky concrete?

PRACTICAL CAT. Idiot!

PUFF-PUFF. What?

PRACTICAL CAT. I said, "IDIOT."

KITTEN. Yeah, I've got to agree. Should have hid it better. Or left it out in the open and blamed the dog. *(Laughs and waves at the group of dogs.)* Didn't you have a litter box?

PUFF-PUFF. I did, one teeny little box clear down in the far corner of the basement in the laundry room, under a counter.

KITTEN. Sounds like a trap.

PUFF-PUFF. Tell me about it! No way to scope out enemy approaches from a horrible dinky-dog. And my person kept forgetting to scoop. They don't make cat-size gas masks, and I couldn't hold my breath and be creative at the same time. I could barely turn around in that teeny toilet without my nether regions hanging out.

PRACTICAL CAT. I like one box for solids and another for liquids, ya know?

PUFF-PUFF. (Dreamily) That sounds like heaven, so to speak...

PRACTICAL CAT. As it were...

PUFF-PUFF. So I crossed my furry legs as long as I could before the planter seduced me. And just as I assumed the position, BAM! I got smacked with a shoe, and was out on my ear, and in mid-euphoria, too. I had to finish on the lawn! On the lawn!! Well, I don't hafta to tell you how humiliating THAT was.

PRACTICAL CAT. Oh, sing me another sad song.

KITTEN. Yeah, me, too. You had it made, Dino, or, should I say, "Dummo."

PUFF-PUFF. You two should talk! You had two boxes and still couldn't hit the mark!

PRACTICAL CAT. Three boxes. 1+1 rule, one box per cat, plus one. (*Defensively*) It wasn't our fault.

S/HE kept guarding the box and wouldn't let me near the facilities. . .

KITTEN. Don't blame me. It was that *(spit)* dog. I really don't like dogs.

PUPPY. (*Hurt*) Hey, I thought we were friends.

HOUND DOG. Sure, blame it on the dog. The dog's always a good patsy.

PUFF-PUFF. For once you're right. (*to other cats*) The dog outsmarted two cats? Really? Talk about humiliating. You want to tell me how a goof-ball dog made you snub the facilities? *(laughing)*

PUPPY. (*whispering to HOUND DOG*) Maybe cats don't like dogs grazing, you know, from the litter box. Isn't that how you lost your home? (*looks at other DOGS*) And you talked about chewing, and digging, and barking--

NAPOLEON. Nothing wrong with chewing, digging and barking. At least we don't crap in the planter.

HOUND DOG. Yeah, and our tails never lie. Cats wag an invitation for a sniff, then BAM! we get nailed with concealed cat weapons.

PRACTICAL CAT. (*Offended*) Cats don't wag. If a nosy dog can't understand a warning tail thump, you deserve what you get!

KITTEN. Wait a minute!

PUPPY. Listen to us!

KITTEN. Stop pointing paws at each other. We all lost homes for the same reason.

PUPPY. We must have done something *really bad.* Wish I knew what I did.

NAPOLEON. *(hanging head)* For a while I thought my name was "bad dog."

PRACTICAL CAT. My person used to call me "Kitty-Stop-That."

KITTEN. Some of you want a second chance. I want a first chance at a forever home so help a kitten out.
PUPPY. Yeah. Think back, what were you doing just before—you know—you got kicked to the curb?

IT'S TIME (STRAYS)

The scene plays on a bare stage. No "animals" are seen. The stage is blue, and the only set pieces are a table, a catch-pole (pole with a rope attached) and a syringe. Alternatively, project the image on a screen—Video is available.

OLD GRUFF (VO1). Who...who's gonna adopt a three-legged dog.
BASSET. What's that?
OLD GRUFF. I said, "Who's gonna adopt a three-legged dog?
MUTT. Knock it off. I'm trying to sleep.
YOUNG VOICE (VO2). I don't even know how I got here. I was just walking along, and this man with a long pole put a rope around my neck, and here I am. Minding my own business, and—
BASSET. "Three legs" you say... Try going around with one eye. One eye and a chewed up ear.
MUTT. Now, THAT'LL sure make someone want to take you home with 'em.
YOUNG VOICE. What is this place? Are they going to help us?
MUTT. Oh, they're going to help you, OK. They're going to help you right into the--
OLD GRUFF. Shut up. Don't scare him.

MUTT. What are there, four of us left? There were seven or eight?

YOUNG VOICE. Seven or eight what?

BASSET. Never mind. Don't listen to them.

YOUNG VOICE. But I want to know--

BASSET. No you don't.

OLD GRUFF. Did you know that I spent most of my life outside? I was tied to a fence, and had a cardboard box to live in. Did you ever watch snow bleed through a cardboard box? Yeah...I've been tied to fences, trees, an old tire.

BASSET. Try having some drunk "teach you a lesson" because you barked too much.

OLD GRUFF. You know how I lost my leg?

YOUNG VOICE. An accident of some kind?

OLD GRUFF. Sure, kid...if being thrown out of a moving car is an accident.

YOUNG VOICE. You're scaring me.

BASSET. He's right. Let's just try to get some rest, if we can--

MUTT. Rest. In here? We'll all be resting before long.

YOUNG VOICE. When we get out of here, maybe we can all just roam around together. Maybe we can find some place where we can--

OLD GRUFF. Sure, kid. We'll all roam around together. We'll eat sirloin steak, and we'll live in a big house. We'll have someone nice to toss a ball for us to chase--

BASSET. And, we'll have a soft dog bed to sleep in, too. That'd be nice. And, how about a lot of soft dirt so we can dig holes and bury soup bones?

MUTT. And, how about a big old cat to chase? Not to catch him or hurt him, but just to chase once in a while.

YOUNG VOICE. That sounds good! And, someone to pet us a lot. And, scratch our ears, too. And, and maybe under our chins.

BASSET. Nah...the side of the face. No, even better! A big old tummy rub! Now, that's living at its best. Nothing's better than a tummy--*Sound of a door opens and then closes.*

YOUNG VOICE. What was that?

MUTT. That was Old Gruff, son. It's his time.

YOUNG VOICE. Time for what?

BASSET. In about five minutes... Well, Old Gruff's gonna have all four of his legs, again. He's gonna be eating sirloin steaks, and he's gonna be digging holes, burying those soup bones...

MUTT. And, he'll be getting those tummy rubs, and having his face scratched. I can just see him chasing that old cat around real soon, now.

BASSET. You rest now, son... Before too long we're all gonna see Old Gruff, and what a time we'll have...what a time.

PIANO MAN (STARZ)

(On dark stage, in spotlight, noodling on piano...monologue with offstage voices.)

REHEARSAL PIANIST. Why people love me, why they should fear me, I'm the glue that holds everything together…

I started piano lessons when I was 5. You'd never know it now, but I had to work really hard at it—my folks just thought it was something to pass the time. Bu you see, it really mattered to me. To do it right. To be really good at something.

I'm not there yet, but still trying.

Do you recognize this song? Of course not. It's an original. I don't get many chances to play my own stuff.

I figure I've played (*plays ~30 second riff of TOMORROW from Annie*), 2126 times, but who's counting? And I smile, and I nod, and I play, and I watch every kid in town with a brand new red wig try to sing it. And tomorrow never comes.

Don't get me wrong, I love what I do. But every once in a while a musician needs a rest. Get it? Oh never mind.

DIRECTOR. Hey [name] we need you to stay late. And the song's too high for [name] so could you write it down a couple steps? Thanks!

REHEARSAL PIANIST. *(he plays heavy handed TOMORROW but in minor key)*

Here's what you might not understand. I play in the orchestra, but also for every rehearsal. The solos usually are fine, because I get to play the written accompaniment. But the chorus rehearsals can fall flat. Get it? Okay, never mind.

See, the chorus stuff has lots of lines to learn, sometimes with singers who don't read music, or can't reach the notes. So who gets to play all the parts in a new order? *(celebration chord—a "ta-da" D-major)*

CHOREOGRAPHER. Hey [name] the dance needs to go faster, a LOT faster!

REHEARSAL PIANIST. That's right. It's the dance stuff, too. *(plays TOMORROW really fast)*

DIRECTOR. Yeah, go faster on that part.

REHEARSAL PIANIST. Which part?

DIRECTOR. You know, that part that's in that deal. That thing we were going over the other night. It was something about, I don't know, I don't remember, but you know, that part. That should be faster.

REHEARSAL PIANIST. (*under his breath*) Not exactly a Juliard graduate.

STAGE MOM. My daughter worked 2 years at Casa Manana . . .

REHEARSAL PIANIST. (*under breath*) probably with lines like, "Milk Duds are 50-cents, and the large box is 75-cents. Would you care for a cold drink?"

STAGE MOM. Your introduction to her song must be SPECIAL, to show case her extraordinary voice.

REHEARSAL PIANIST. (*plays the worms crawl in the works crawl out…*) Oh, and here comes the vocal coach. S/he at least understands music. Mostly. I've worked with some great vocal coaches. And then some that . . .

VOCAL COACH. You're playing too LOUD. Except at measure 297, and the pick up to 586 is too fast, and I want the adagio faster, and play song #12 sort of…you know…slithery.

REHEARSAL PIANIST. (*plays TOMORROW like a march*) Something else you may not know. People like me, we're rarely paid, unless you get to the pro level. Like I said, I started taking lessons when I was five, so that means I've been playing [how many years]. Pianists may have full time jobs, maybe teaching, or rushing from playing for the church to get to a matinee performance on time. Going to class during the day getting a degree. Or taking care of our own kids. And if we get sick well, the show must go on. There's no understudy for the piano player. Sure, they've got those audio recording tracks now and they work great for some rehearsals but for me—nothing beats live music.

VOCALIST. Hey man, wanted to thank you for saving my bacon. Don't know how I missed that entrance, but the audience never knew—it was seamless. You're a lifesaver, a true pro!

REHEARSAL PIANIST. *(long pause)* A recording couldn't do that. And you wonder why I do this? Enough said.

PERFECT (STARZ)

UNISON. I'm perfect. They're not. (*pointing at each other*)

INGENUE. Look at me: beautiful hair, gorgeous eyes, and get a load of this profile. (*gestures to whole body*)

LEADING MAN. Look at me: beautiful hair, gorgeous eyes, and get a load of this profile. (*strikes pose to side*)

STAGE HOG. *(gets in between them, belches loudly)* And get a load of me. After I burped, all you're thinking about is me.

INGENUE. I'm poetry in motion—comes from years of ballet and jazz.

LEADING MAN. Ladies swoon when I enter a room—comes from years of body sculpting--

STAGE HOG. …and implants. Me, I'm au natural, doncha love it? *(poses)* But seriously, I'm perfect, too. Ya gotta own it. Am I right?

LEADING MAN. My voice gives the audience chills.

STAGE HOG. So does mine.

INGENUE. Singing has always come natural to me. (*sings an arpeggio*)

STAGE HOG. Dancing is my forte (*dances…badly*)

LEADING MAN. Really, don't be jealous of me. I'm generous to the lesser folk, if they'd just watch and learn.

INGENUE. You can't teach me anything. I was born perfect.

LEADING MAN. I happen to have an agent.

INGENUE. I have an agent, too.

STAGE HOG. I'm my own stage mother. (*to Leading Man*) How do you get a part?

LEADING MAN. Talent and preparation.

STAGE HOG. Preparation H? For the H of it?

LEADING MAN. (*steps back as though preparing...*) "What light in yon window breaks? It is the East and Juliet is the sun."

STAGE HOG. (*to girl*) And what do YOU do to get the part?

INGENUE. Besides talent and preparation? Hairspray and lip gloss. "Just last week I talked Beyonce out of buying a truly heinous cable-knit tube top! Whoever said tangerine was the new pink was seriously disturbed!" (*Opens purse, applies lip gloss*)

LEADING MAN. (to Stage Hog) What do you do to get a part?

STAGE HOG. (*all action happens very quickly: falls on floor, "walks" in circle on side, stands up, speaks bombastic*) "All the world's a stage…." (sings) "The sun'll come out tomorrow." (*burps*) I'll do anything to get the part.

INGENUE LEADING MAN. Does that work?

STAGE HOG. I booked three jobs last week, without an agent. What have you booked lately?

LEADING MAN. I need to call my agent.

INGENUE. I need a new color lip gloss.

STAGE HOG. Don't hate them cuz they're perfect.

BABY NAMES (KURVES)

MAXINE. *(Noticing from across the room)* Jane? Janie? Are you OK? Are you all right, sweetie?

JANE. (*Quickly wiping tears away*) I'm fine. It's these new eye drops. They kinda--

RONNIE. She'll be fine. Nothing a little workout won't fix. Right Jane? *(JANE doesn't respond)* I said, "Right, Jane?" *(Quietly)* Come on; don't let 'em see you like this. We'll talk later. Besides, we've got a deal.

JANE. *(Recovering)* Oh right. Exercise is my middle name. Because I've got my class reunion and you've got that date with a baby.

RONNIE. (*Whispering to JANE)* Hush on the baby stuff. *(To MAXINE*) She's fine. We're both fine.

MABEL. Well hallelujah, all's right with the Lord. Now Maxine, can you get us some decent music?

MAXINE. I could sing you a bit of *Jesus Loves Me*... (*JANE and RONNIE laugh*)

MABEL. Ronnie, do you have names picked out? If it's a boy, I've always loved the name Roscoe.

MAXINE. Roscoe?

MABEL. I always had a huge crush on Roscoe Karnes.

MAXINE. Who is Roscoe Karnes?

MABEL. I loved him on TV back in the 50s.

MAXINE. No one remembers TV in the 50s, except you.

RONNIE. I'm not naming my child Roscoe. I had a Chihuahua named Roscoe. He was small, wormy, and shook all the time.

MABEL. So did Roscoe Karnes, but I still loved him.

JANE. You could name him after your husband—Troy Chadwick Noonan. The fifth? You could always call him Chad to cut down on the confusion factor.

RONNIE. Yes, that could be a problem. At family reunions, you call for Troy and every man in the place turns his head.

MAXINE. Mabel, you're Baptist, aren't you? You know what they say about Baptists—wherever you find four Baptists, you find a fifth.

MABEL. That's not funny. Well, it is funny but I'm not allowed to laugh at such things. Rev. Calvin wouldn't like it.

MAXINE. Calvin's dead.

MABEL. Don't tell him.

RONNIE. Don't say fifth. That's where Mom gets all her great ideas. (*She mimes drinking.*) But if it's a boy, for sure it'll be another Troy.

JANE. What about girl names?

MABEL. How about Heddy?

RONNIE. Heady? No disrespect, Mabel, but what are you thinking?

MABEL. Heddy Lamar. Wasn't she the most beautiful thing you ever saw?

MAXINE. No one besides Heddy Lamar was ever named Heddy.

MABEL. Heddy Troy Noonan the first.

MAXINE. Mabel, did anyone ever tell you your butt looks big?

JANE. My cat has a toy mouse without the head. (*They look at her, she shrugs*) I found the head buried in her box. I never saw Heddy Lamar. Just trying to make conversation.

RONNIE. (*To herself*) I got to get pregnant first . . .

MABEL. You can name her Eugenia after my grandmother. She died forty years ago. You've all seen her picture over my mantel.

MAXINE. Yes we did Mabel. Ugliest woman I ever saw. Been buried forty years you say? Probably looks better now.

RONNIE. Enough with the names! Can't we change the subject?

JANE. She's right. Why get all concerned over something that—

RONNIE. Any baby is going to be named whatever Troy's mother says, anyway. You know her. Helen Noonan says it and it becomes "Noonan family law." If I had my way, I'd name it Sissulfuss just to spite her.

MABEL. Sissulfuss Noonan...Do you have a middle name picked out?

MAXINE. Mabel, please.

RONNIE. You've all known her for years. Driving around Kurves, Texas in her big, black Lincoln. Looking down her nose at everyone. Do you know the first thing she ever said to me? Do you? She always uses that awful supercilious tone. *(Mimicking Helen's tone)* "You realize, dear—Veronica, is it?—that Troy has never dated a heavy girl before." *(Starts to cry quietly)* And, Troy just stood there. Finally, he told her that we were going out to dinner, and she looked me up and down. Then she told Troy, "Well, I hope you brought plenty of money."

JANE. Ronnie, please don't—

RONNIE. Me and the town's catch—that was Mom's idea, did I tell you? *(Mimics mom)* "Marry the town prince, the town Adonis, Ronnie, and get set for life." But I really love him, and he loves me, at least I think he does. He just can't stand up to Helen.

(Confessing) I wasn't pregnant, but I told him I was. (*Ladies look shocked*) Another one of Mom's ideas *(pantomimes taking a shot)*. Can you believe we were still in the courtroom when she came up with that. Why did I listen to her? Now I've got to get pregnant. I don't want to lose him!

JANE. Courtroom?

RONNIE. Troy was prosecuting Mom for her second DWI. That's how I met him. *(Sarcastic)* Damn romantic, isn't it? (*(looks at MABEL)* Sorry for the language.

JANE. He loves you. I know he does.

RONNIE. *(Angry)* How? How do you know? Are you there? Do you see him looking at me like maybe he's made a mistake? You think I don't see him look at other women when he thinks I don't notice?

MAXINE. All guys do that. It's in their nature. All of them have the stupidity gene, and all of them look. They have this brain that shifts from their heads to other places. I hate to say it, but they're just wired to be stupid, sometimes.

MABEL. Well, luckily, women are different. We don't make mistakes…

MAXINE. Right, Mabel. Four husbands is it?

MABEL. Now, I won't listen to that kind of talk. My husbands were all--

MAXINE. Yeah, I know. Comfortable.

RONNIE. We're all stupid. Maybe I am more than anyone.

TOO LATE FOR SORRY (KURVES)

CELIA. Thirty years is a long time, Max. Life goes on. I've been married and divorced since then. I can't just pick up where we left off. Even if I wanted to. And I don't.

MAX. To say "I'm sorry" isn't enough, is it?

CELIA. Doesn't even come close.

MAX. You want to talk about it?

CELIA. Not really. What's the use, it won't make any difference now, anyway.

MAX. Nothing that's happened to you could be nearly as bad as what's happened to me.

CELIA. Why you son-of-a…(*Looks around, consciously lowers her voice. It's measured, full of venom, purposely hurtful).* Like I said before, I made myself. Complete with body armor, so I'd never get hurt again the way you hurt me. You even gave me my new name. (*Pulls out ring and reads inscription) "To the LOVE--JOY of my life."* Steven Seidleman, my manager, wanted to be more than that and I tried. Hell, he did everything for me, got me bookings, the TV show, he gave me everything. I owed him. So we got married. He made me me, and I made him miserable. I kept comparing him to you, to this fantasy person who was never real. We lasted seven months. Probably longer than we would have lasted. He's a better manager than husband, and I'm a better "self made me" than a wife. I wasn't meant to be a wife. You did me a favor when you disappeared.

MAX. I did you a favor by not marrying you.

CELIA. We finally agree on something.

MAX. I didn't marry you for all the right reasons. And you married him for all the wrong ones.

CELIA. At least I was there, and told him to his face.

RONNIE. *(Interjecting)* What is wrong with you people?

CELIA. Stay out of it, this is none of your business.

RONNIE. You think there's a statute of limitations on loving someone?

CELIA. There is in my world.

RONNIE. Then you're in the wrong world. *(To MAX)* You didn't marry for the right reasons before? So what's stopping you now? Do it for the right reasons this time—you don't need to throw it away a second time. *(Looks toward Jane)* High school reunions are full of people who are looking for second chance love, and it never works, because you can't go back in time. Don't you realize that the two of you actually have a chance here? You never had your first chance—so this is your first chance. Don't turn your back on it.

MAX. I'd love to give it a chance, if she wasn't so pig-headed. That at least hasn't changed! It's hard to work with one-sided willingness.

CELIA. You're the one who slammed the door, with that sorry excuse for a reason. At least be a man and own up to--

RONNIE. Stop it! What does the reason matter? *(To MAX)* Do you love her?

MAX. I never stopped.

RONNIE. Celia, did you ever stop loving Max?

CELIA. I made myself stop. I'm in the business of convincing myself and others. I'm very good at it.

MAX. So if you want to, you can convince yourself that we can still work?

CELIA. It's not that easy. Why would I want to?

YOU WRITE CRAP (RADIO DAZE)

BENNY. *(practicing, vocalizing/warm up for news stories, spray throat, awful voice)* To be or not to be . . . *(clears throat, and makes notes on a paper on the desk).* Headlining the news today, Fern Wilkensen has reported three of her best laying hens stolen. Fern says, and I quote, "Someone took them layers, leavin' me with egg all over my face. I hate a thief, and a chicken thief is the worst. If you're out there, chicken thief, I'm a-comin' for ya." This reporter warned her that assault and battery with a frying pan could get her 30 days. Let's hope that Fern finds those fryers fast.

ROB. *(chickens clucking sound. BENNY glares).* Just trying to make your boring news more exciting. Sound effects are the punctuation marks of radio.

PEARL. *(enters, watching)*

BENNY. In other news, Abigail Abercrombie continues to improve in the local hospital after suffering smoke inhalation. She refuses to give up her smokes, though, and says (and I quote), "I'd rather fight, than switch."

ROB. *(coughing/wheezing sound)*

BENNY. And now a word from our sponsor. *(sees PEARL).* Do you mind? I'm rehearsing here.

PEARL. Aren't you Benny Kornblat? I cannot believe you're still here! Your show was a national radio broadcast! I'll never forget what you said when the Hindenberg blew up. Everyone remembers, "Oh the humanity!" But you said,

BENNY. *(talking to her)* Boy, that's a lot of hot air.

PEARL. Yes, you said it just like that! I've got chills.

BENNY. The worst part about that tragedy, my car was parked right below that damn blimp. I loved that car. Now, what do you want, girly? I'm busy uncovering the news of the day.

PEARL. I need your Underwood.

BENNY. Well, I don't like to brag but...junior here--

PEARL. Your typewriter. I've got a script to finish.

BENNY. We're both writers. Only I write real life, and you write crap.

PEARL. Fiction reflects real life, don't give me that holier than thou schmaltz. Or I'll write and then kill off your character. (*to herself*) I need some kind of poignant moment to pull everything to a climax. I want the audience to laugh and cry, to tug their heartstrings.

BENNY. Did you hear my story about the stolen chickens?

PEARL. Weren't you on your way out?

BENNY. (*a beat*) Yes, I'm afraid so. (*wads up papers, tosses in wastebasket and exits*)

PEARL. (*fishes wadded paper out of wastebasket*) Hey, not bad! (*starts typing*)

SNAZZY. (*enters*) Hey Pearl, you're a big-time writer, I wanna try out my latest ad on you. (*clears throat and reads/chants from paper*).

COME TO BERNIE'S SHOP AND SWAP.
C'MON YOU SHOPPERS,
IT'S WORTH A STOP.
BELIEVE ME WE'VE GOT
JUST WHAT YOU NEED,
FROM REAL NICE RADIOS
TO CHICKEN FEED.
WE'LL SEE YOU AT BERNIE'S
DAY OR NIGHT.

WHERE YA GET A DEAL,
AND WE DO IT RIGHT.
COME ON IN
FOR A SHOPAPALOOZA,
CUZ A REAL GREAT DEAL
IS WHAT WE'LL DOOZ YA!

YEAH, BERNIE'S, YEAH, BERNIE'S,
YEAH, BERNIE'S.... *(fade out)*

PEARL. *(nods off during ad)*
SNAZZY. I'll take that as a maybe. *(exits)*
ROB. *(wha-wha-whaaaaaa disappointment sound).*

HOLD THAT THOUGHT (RADIO DAZE)

> *BOB plays from his office while WILADINE from Irving's office, SPOT on each of them. PEARL runs back and forth between.*

BOB. This presents a major problem for me. For years I've wanted to get out from under this albatross of a station. At this point, there's no joy in what I do.
PEARL. Is that really how you feel?
BOB. Yes. And that's what scares me.
PEARL. Have you given any consideration to the people who work here?
BOB. No. I mean, yes. No I really haven't –well I mean, yes I have. Benny's been with me for 30 years, and he brought in Irving.

PEARL. What about Wiladine?

BOB. What about Wiladine? She's only been here what? Three years, I think. Feels like forever, though.

PEARL. Do you have any idea how much she actually does around here? WPDQ would have folded five years ago, without her plugging away. She answers the phone, books appointments, invoices sponsors, and even scrubs the damn toilets.

BOB. I never thought about that. She's my right hand man. Except she's a woman, of course.

PEARL. Hold that thought. *(crosses to WILADINE)* Have you given any thought about what to do after—I mean, when the station sells?

WILADINE. Don't you mean, IF the station sells?

PEARL. Sure, whatever, IF it sells.

WILADINE. My brother invited me to work with him. He sells Crosley Hotshots, the car of the future. Everyone wants one. *(depressed)*

PEARL. Sounds good. But what would you really like to do?

WILADINE. You mean, my dream? Well, I'd love to retire to a sweet little cabana in Cuba, with a nice fella. If I had the funds. And the cabana. And the fella. Course, all that's scarce as hen's teeth. Not that it matters, but do you know what your Uncle Bob's plans are? I mean, IF the station sells?

PEARL. That's a good question. Hold that thought. *(crosses back to BOB)* So Uncle Bob, what's your plan if the station sells?

BOB. You mean WHEN it sells? My dream is to visit a little island where life's slow, the music's hot, and the company's sweet. You know, like the song said, I never had a wife. Maybe it's too late. But I'd settle for buying a Crosley Hotshot and touring the country.

PEARL. Tour the country? By yourself? Sounds lonely.

BOB. (pause) I've spent most of my life lonely. Except when I'm here, in the middle of these crazies. Wiladine's the only one keeps the crazy to a dull roar.

PEARL. Hold that thought. (*cross to WILADINE, looks at her, starts to say something then...she's got nothing*). Hold that thought. *(returns to BOB)*

ABOUT THE SHOWS

Monologues, duo and group scenes have been excerpted with permission from four productions written and produced by SHOJAI & STEELE PLAYS. All are available for licensing, and musicals include rehearsal/performance CDs. More information including video excerpts can be reviewed at http://amyshojai.com/plays.

A COMFORT BREEZE, Drama in 3 Acts (2W).

In a shabby West Texas hotel in the summer of 1993, Joetta meets Audie, the baby she gave up for adoption 27 years ago. Life has not been kind to Joetta, but she's relieved to see Audie's obvious success. Far from being grateful, Audie's cold resentment puzzles and then angers Joetta, and she's disappointed their reunion is anything but rainbows and hugs she'd hoped. The two women verbally dance around the reality of each other's lives during one long sweltering afternoon of drinks, off-color stories, resentment and tears. The mix of hilarious-to-heart-wrenching dialogue shakes them both to their core—This mother-daughter reunion demands very strong actors for a performance that will bring audiences to their feet. ***Adult themes & language.***

KURVES, THE MUSICAL (4M, 4W).

A two-hour musical comedy in two acts, featuring 12 songs and eight actors onstage virtually the whole time. The play is set in Kurves, Texas and takes place early one morning when a group of misfits get locked inside a woman's gym. Despite failed attempts to find happiness they finally succeed—but in unexpected ways.

In **ACT ONE**, we learn that wise-cracking Maxine (played by a man) has owned the gym for 30 years. Three regulars arrive. Mabel is the many-times-married director of a soup kitchen who despite her drill-sergeant demeanor is a softie who collects human strays needing help. Old maid poetry teacher Jane wants to make an impression at her next high school reunion because she's always felt invisible (song: **SOMEONE MUST SEE ME**). Newlywed Ronnie from the wrong side of the tracks married the "town catch" Troy but lied about being pregnant and feels unworthy of his love (song: **THE PICTURE**).

Two inept small-time thieves, Boots and Fingers, attempt to rob the women. Boots fancies himself a dancer and ladies' man and wants a fancy car to attract the woman of his dreams. Fingers carries his treasures in his Superman lunchbox and has always been the butt of jokes but just wants a purpose in life (song/duet: **PITCHING WOO**). The pair cut the phone line, tape up the women and deposit swiped jewelry into Finger's lunchbox while Boots hits on the women with groaner pick-up lines (song/dance: **YOU'RE THE CHICK FOR ME**).

Quizzed about a mysterious past, Maxine reveals a long-ago love disappeared when life threw unexpected curves (song: **CURVES**). After glitzy bitchy visitor Celia arrives at the gym for a workout, Boots locks the door to prevent future interruptions and breaks the key, trapping everyone inside. Fingers and Boots exit to try and get out the jammed back door.

Celia is recognized as a famous TV motivational speaker. She gives Jane and Ronnie a pep talk (song/trio: **DREAMS FOR SALE**), but Celia admits to herself that she's tired of being a fake, but doesn't know how to stop. Meanwhile Maxine recognizes Celia as his lost love but fears revealing the truth.

When Boots and Fingers return to the stage the women tie them up. Celia reclaims her "sparkles" and Fingers recognizes her ring-necklace matches Maxine's—and the jig is up when Celia recognizes Max as her long-lost fiancé. In the finale, each character complains the others "have it better" (song/company: **LIFE HAPPENS**). Maxine becomes Max when he removes his wig, shocking everyone that he's a man, just as the lights go down.

ACT TWO opens with Celia anguished by Max's betrayal. She laments her lost 30 years and demands an explanation (song/duet: **THE DREAM**). Mabel gets fed up with everyone's pity party complaints, and all but Celia "confess" and receive gospel-style pep talks from Mabel (song/Company: **SUCK IT UP, SWEETHEART**).

Max explains his disappearance and begs for another chance with Celia. But after 30 years of silence, she can't trust his story that he disappeared to protect her. The previous gym owner wouldn't sell to a man so he masqueraded as a woman to hide from the mob because "that's how witness protection works."

Mabel wants to help lovable simple Fingers but without insulting him (song/duet: **PITCHING WOO**, reprise) when he explains movies help him find the right words (song: **SILVER SCREEN BLUES**). Fingers agrees to take a job at the soup kitchen to help kids find and recognize their own treasures.

Jane and Boots are smitten, delighted to find each other and that finally someone "sees" and appreciates them. Jane agrees to help Boots become more refined if he'll teach her how to put jazz in her life (song/duet: **POETRY & JAZZ**).

Ronnie the romantic scolds Celia for not accepting a "real life fairytale come true" when they've actually got a second chance at love. Celia wants to give Max (and herself) one more chance (song: **AM I HAPPY?**) but fears being hurt again.

Ronnie's husband TROY bursts through the back door, looking for his wife—he knows the trick for opening the lock. Ronnie fearfully admits she's not pregnant, but he doesn't care, and professes his love (song/duet: **THE PICTURE**, reprise). He's the assistant DA and tells about just recovered mob money that's been traced to the mafia hit man Max testified against 30 years ago. They learn that Max could have come out of hiding 15 years earlier. Celia realizes Max's outrageous story is true.

Fingers asks if Celia and Max will reconcile after all these years (song/company: **CURVES** reprise). Everyone prepares to go home—in couples—and Celia admits she's already home. She gives Jane her sparkly coat as she's "out grown it" so Jane truly becomes the girl with the sparkles. The entire company discovers they finally grabbed and caught the brass ring (song/company: **LIFE HAPPENS**, reprise).

STARZ, THE MUSICAL

is inspired by attendees of the Texas Thespian Festivals, and is a two-hour musical in two acts featuring 12 songs. It is written especially for theater lovers, and explores the many ways performers and supporters come to the stage, with the attendant joys, frustrations, hopes and dreams that keep them there. The actors give voice to a variety of theater "types" –singers, dancers, drama mommas and directors, clueless dads and jealous boyfriends, ingénue pros and shy amateurs, stage managers and stage hogs, tech crew and more--in this funny, poignant, and ultimately uplifting next generation "chorus line" that allows each to share their journey as they reach for the **STARZ.**

This is a review format show designed to be mounted in a bare (or minimal set) performance area. It may be cast with as few as 6-8 performers doubling roles, or 16 featured performers plus chorus. A mix of body types, ages and genders is available, with casting against "type" encouraged.

STRAYS, THE MUSICAL is a two-hour musical in two acts with 12 songs, and can be performed on a bare stage or elaborate sets. It is written especially with pet lovers in mind and explores furry foibles from the PETS' point of view. The actors give voice to a variety of cat and dog characters in this hilarious and often moving "drama-dy" that seeks to edu-tain audiences about normal pet behavior while honoring the bond we share with pets. The complete show runs approximately two hours with an intermission. It can be performed with or without a break.

STRAYS is a review format show, with a mix of funny to poignant scenes (with and without music) designed to be modular. That is, it can be licensed for performance using only the cat-specific, dog-specific or general (both) content that best suits the audience. The authors hope it will be widely used in pet-specific fund-raising efforts.

STRAYS can be cast with any age performer, but age 14 to adult is recommended. It is important that actors have at least like pets—this empathy is vital to the success of the show and cannot be faked. Actors can be encouraged to create their own cat/dog characters based on the scenes/songs they will perform, including "naming" their characters to replace generic names when not otherwise specified. The **PARIAH CAT**, **PUPPY** and **KITTEN** characters remain constant throughout the show; other actors may create a different character in each scene, as you wish. This is an ensemble show, with no specific "stars" and all actors onstage throughout the performance.

A mix of body types, ages and genders offers the most fun and flexibility, as well as reflecting the message that pets also come in all shapes, sizes, personalities, ages and looks. The "type" of character (dog or cat, specific breed, young or old, etc.) should come primarily from the actor's actions and cued from the dialogue.

The show can be mounted with as few as **EIGHT ADULT SINGER/ACTORS** doubling roles, or **25+ FEATURED PLAYERS** plus a **CHORUS** that may include young performers as puppies and kittens. Suggested casting/doubling recommendations follow, but songs and scenes may be mixed and matched to best fit talents.

RADIO DAZE, THE 1940s MUSICAL

is a funny and often touching homage to the late 1940s. The story unfolds in the failing WPDQ radio station. The owner, Bob Hope (the one from Schenectady) is ready to cut his losses and sell out to the latest fad–television. A motley crew of staff, has-been movie stars, and strangers off the street come together to try and save the station–and fail miserably to hilarious effect. Cast with 6M/6W, **RADIO DAZE** is the perfect date night or family-friendly-evening-out event. The two-hour show will leave you laughing, humming catchy tunes, and hugging your loved ones close.

RADIO DAZE is an ensemble show appropriate for any age performer, from high school to professional venues. Characters include station owner BOB HOPE (the one from Schenectady), his love-sick assistant WILADINE, the director IRVING, grumpy news guy BENNY, and girl Friday, DOTTIE. Bob hires his niece PEARL to write a script. Irving hires sound effects guy ROB, salesman SNAZZY to sell ads, and has-been talents BARRY, his ex-wife DIZZY, and the PEPPER SISTERS (all played by the same actress) to perform. Meanwhile, the mysterious stranger ROSIE hides secrets that could change the station forever.

ABOUT THE PLAYWRIGHTS

Playwrights Amy Shojai and Frank Steele have co-authored several theatrical productions together. Each brings decades of writing and performance experience to the projects.

Frank Steele has appeared in many TV and radio commercials, movies and TV shows including DALLAS. He taught drama for twenty-seven years, including middle school thespians, anStraysCast1d has appeared in over fifty plays as an actor or professional musician, playing drums.

Amy Shojai, although best known as a pet journalist and author, has degrees in theater and music performance. She has acted in several dozen plays in six states, played piano and cello in many productions, and made countless TV and radio appearances both locally and nationally, including Animal Planet appearances as an expert. Amy has also taught high school choir and directed musicals from Chicago and Legally Blonde, to Peter Pan and Beauty & the Beast. Review Amy's acting information here.

Together they write the book of the show, taking turns offering potential dialogue and scene suggestions. Songs arise from the theatrical situation to move the story forward. Shojai and Steele often begin with a concept for the song, each individually write verses or chorus of the proposed song, and then combine them for layered musical effect. Once suggested melodies and instrumentation is agreed, Shojai creates the arrangements. By the final edits, neither can tell who suggested which part once the work is completed.

The productions by SHOJAI & STEELE PLAYS are available for license. Email shojai-steele-plays@shojai.com for further information.

www.ingramcontent.com/pod-product-compliance
Lightning Source LLC
Chambersburg PA
CBHW071538080526
44588CB00011B/1717